...PY

UP IN THE SKY

THE

SUN

BY
TAMRA ORR

Mitchell Lane
PUBLISHERS

P.O. Box 196
Hockessin, Delaware 19707
Visit us on the web: www.mitchelllane.com
Comments? email us:
mitchelllane@mitchelllane.com

The Clouds
The Moon
The Stars
The Sun

Printing   1   2   3   4   5   6   7   8   9

ABOUT THE AUTHOR: Award-winning children's book author Tamra Orr lives with her family in the Pacific Northwest.

Library of Congress Cataloging-in-Publication Data
Orr, Tamra.
 I spy up in the sky the sun / by Tamra Orr.
    p. cm. — (Randy's corner: i spy in the sky)
 Includes bibliographical references and index.
 ISBN 978-1-58415-972-8 (library bound)
 1. Sun — Juvenile literature. I. Title.
 QB521.5.O77 2011
 523.7 — dc22
                                                                                2011000785

eBook ISBN: 9781612281421

                                                                                PLB

I SPY
UP IN THE SKY

THE
SUN

4

Star Light, Star Bright

Can you feel the sunshine
Warming you with its glow?
Its rays of energy
Help all life-forms grow.

The fiery Sun
Is our closest star.
It heats the planet
And sends light from afar.

Center of the Solar System

Mercury

Venus

Earth

Mars

Jupiter

Ceres

Earth circles the Sun
At just the right place.
Too close would be too hot;
Too far, we'd freeze in space.

Saturn

Uranus

Neptune

Pluto

2003 UB$_{313}$

Rise and Shine!

Each day in the east—
If you can believe your eyes—
The sky starts to lighten,
The Sun begins to rise.

It peeks over the horizon
And turns night to day—
Because Earth is turning,
It appears this way.

Worshiping the Sun

Ancient people believed
The Sun was alive.
Some built it temples
To convince it to rise.

They worshiped the star
And stories they made.
They sent sacrifices;
To the Sun they prayed.

Telling Time

The ancient Egyptians
Told time with style.
They marked the Sun's angle
With a sundial.

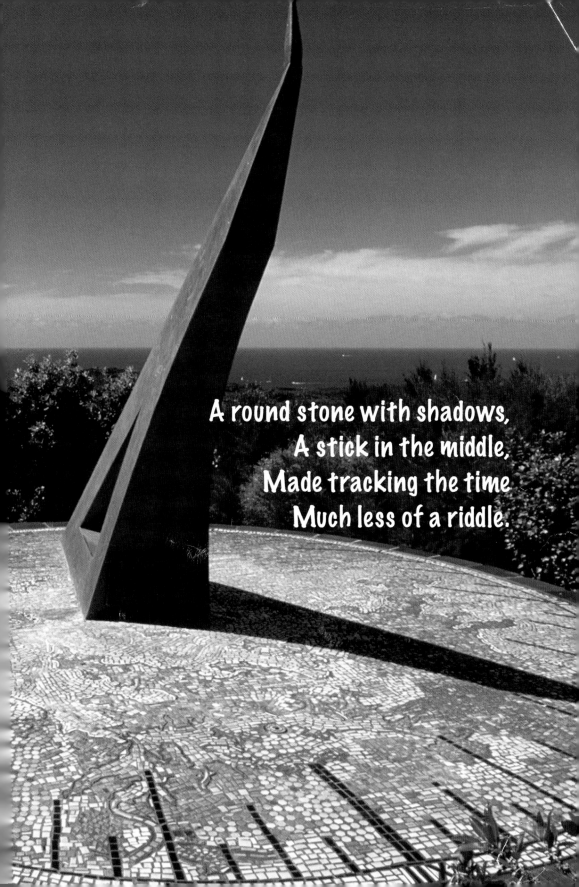

A round stone with shadows,
A stick in the middle,
Made tracking the time
Much less of a riddle.

The Sun's Magic Trick

Occasionally
The Sun disappears.
This solar event
Once caused great fear.

Today we all know
When the Moon gets between
The Sun and the Earth
An eclipse can be seen.

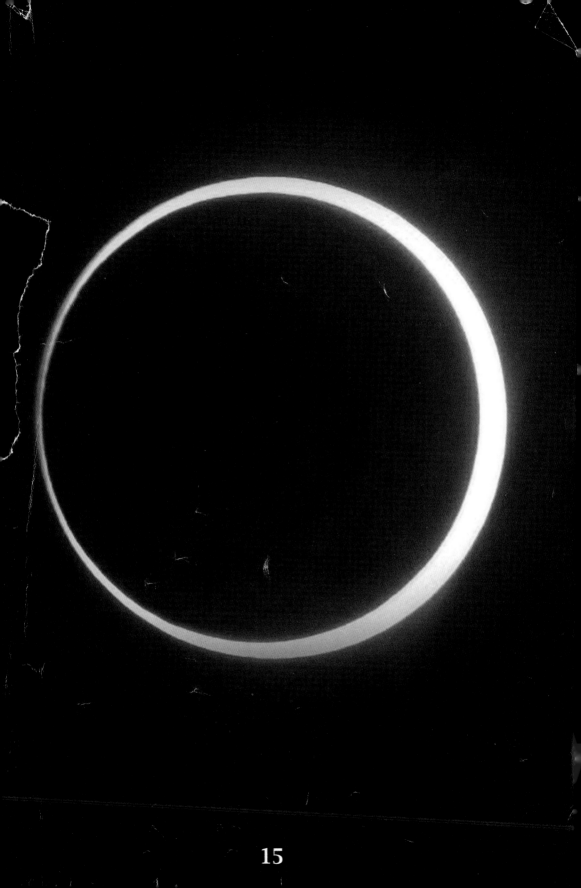

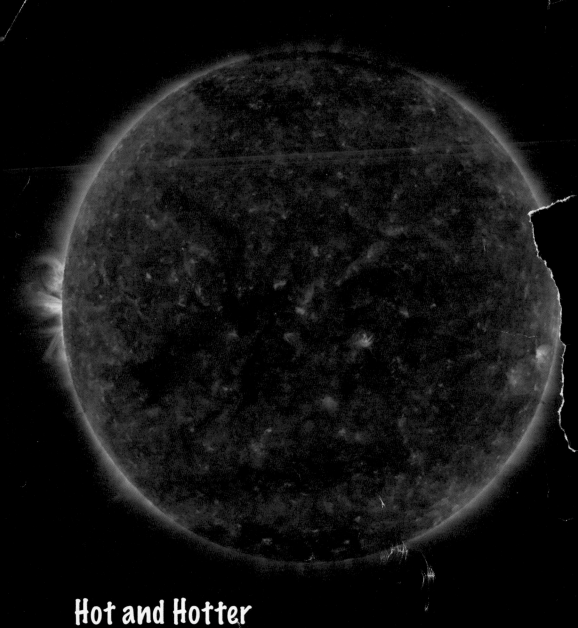

Hot and Hotter

The Sun burns in layers—
The hottest, the core.
Temperatures reach millions
Of degrees—and more!

Up on the surface
It's cooler, agreed.
There it is only
Thousands of degrees!

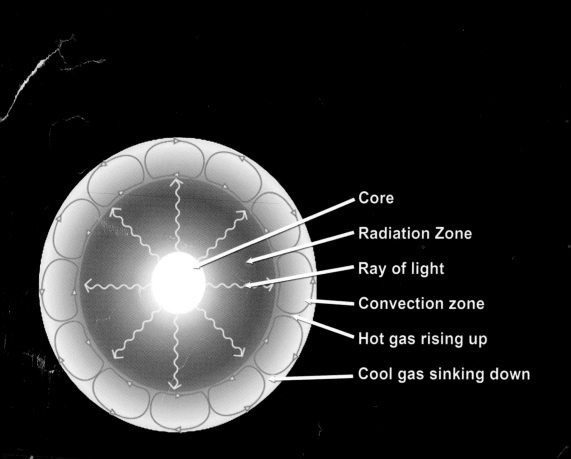

Core

Radiation Zone

Ray of light

Convection zone

Hot gas rising up

Cool gas sinking down

A Solar Crown

Surrounding the sun
Is a crown of light
Called the corona—
An incredible sight.

Time and again
The corona flashes.
For billions of years
It has burned hot gases.

Seeing Spots

Is that a freckle
Up there on the Sun?
Look! More over here—
And another one!

Sunspots are places
The temperature drops.
They're on the surface
Where the corona stops.

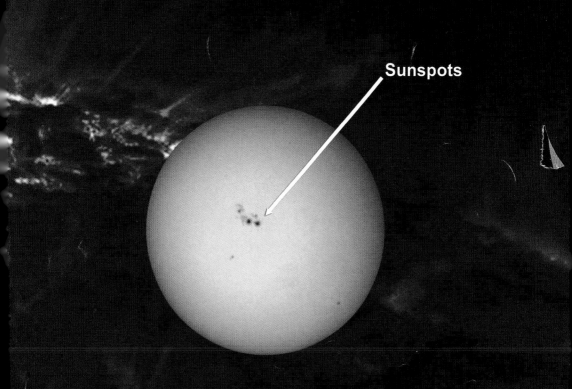

Sunspots

A Flare from Space

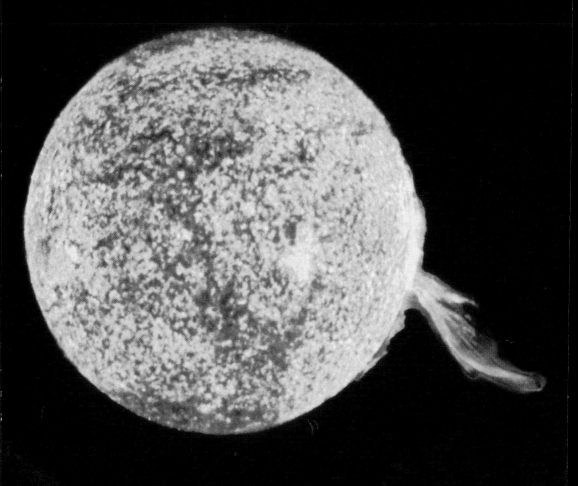

Every now and then
The Sun sends a flare
Like millions of bombs
Exploding up there.

On Earth, we're protected,
But solar flares are known
For knocking out power
And blocking cell phones.

Capturing Sunlight

Einstein discovered
Effects of sunlight
And how it releases
Incredible might.

Now solar panels
Capture sunshine.
We can store its power
To use when it's time.

Into the Sunset

After hours of shining,
Daylight comes to an end;
The Sun sinks in the west
And darkness descends.

As when the Sun rises,
Earth's movement is why
The bright orange Sun
Seems to drop from the sky.

Sunshine on Your Shoulders

Next time you're outside
On a bright sunny day,
Think about how the Sun
Helps you have fun and play.

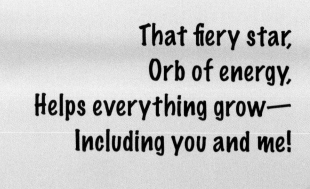

That fiery star,
Orb of energy,
Helps everything grow—
Including you and me!

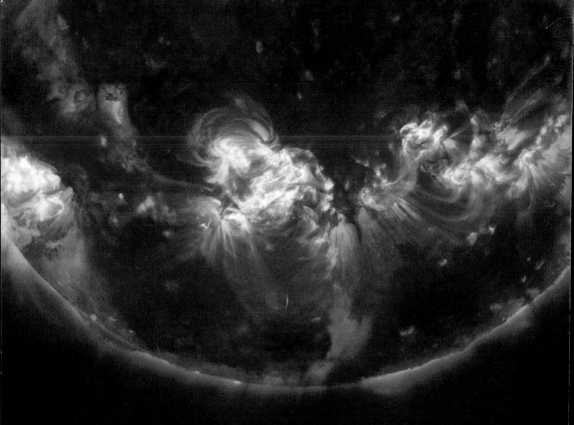

Sun Facts

Approximate age	4.6 billion years
Rotation	27 days
Composition	92 percent hydrogen; 7 percent helium; 1 percent other gases
Surface temperature	10,000°F (5,500°C)
Core temperature	27,000,000°F (15,000,000°C)
Diameter	870,000 miles (1,390,000 kilometers)
Distance from Earth	93,000,000 miles (150,000,000 kilometers)

A special warning here—
Although the Sun looks kind,
If you look without protection,
It can make you blind.

core (KOHR)—The innermost part of the Sun.

corona (kuh-ROH-nuh)—The crown of fire that flares from the Sun's surface.

eclipse (ee-KLIPS)—A short period of time when the Sun becomes dark as the Moon moves between Earth and the Sun.

flare (FLAYR)—An explosion of energy from the Sun's surface.

orbit (OR-bit)—The path that one object makes around a larger object in space.

solar panel (SOH-lur PAN-ul)—A device that turns energy from the Sun into electrical energy.

solar system (SOH-lur SIS-tum)—The Sun and all the other objects that orbit the Sun.

sundial (SUN-dyl)—A device that measures time by tracking a shadow as it moves across its surface.

sunspot (SUN-spot)—A cool area that appears dark on the surface of the Sun.

FURTHER READING

Books

Asch, Frank. *The Sun Is My Favorite Star*. Boston, MA: Sandpiper, 2008.

Chrismer, Melanie. *The Sun*. Mankato, MN: Children's Press, 2008.

Kaner, Etta. *Who Likes the Sun?* Toronto, Ontario: Kids Can Press, 2007.

Paratore, Coleen. *Catching the Sun*. Watertown, MA: Charlesbridge Publishing, 2008.

Swanson, Susan Marie. *To Be Like the Sun*. New York: Harcourt Children's Books, 2008.

Works Consulted

Hewitt, Lyons, Suchocki, and Yeh. *Conceptual Integrated Science*, Chapter 27, "The Solar System." Upper Saddle River, NJ: Pearson Higher Education, 2007.

NASA's Imagine the Universe "The Sun's Corona" http://imagine.gsfc.nasa.gov/docs/science/mysteries_l1/corona.html

World Book at NASA: Sun http://www.nasa.gov/worldbook/sun_worldbook.html

On the Internet

European Space Agency: "The Sun" http://www.esa.int/esaKIDSen/TheSun.html

Explore the Sun: "Facts about our Closest Star" http://www.kidscosmos.org/kid-stuff/sun-facts.html

Kids Astronomy: The Sun http://www.kidsastronomy.com/our_sun.htm

The Nine Planets http://kids.nineplanets.org/portfoli.htm

INDEX

PHOTO CREDITS: Cover—Joe Rasemas; p. 10—AFP/Stringer/Getty Images; p. 12—Anders Blomqvist/Getty Images; p. 16—NASA; p. 20—TRACE; p. 24—Geir Pettersen/Getty Images; p. 28—Cornstock Images/Getty Images. All other photos—CreativeCommons. Every effort has been made to locate all copyright holders of materials used in this book. Any errors or omissions will be corrected in future editions of the book.